To Max,
All I need is your love for
my dreams to come true.

And for my children,
May you always see the
diversity this world has
to offer.

Outside it's dark and dreary, but during this time of year, there are many ways to celebrate cheer.

 is for All-Hallows' Eve.

Also known as Halloween, All-Hallow's Eve is a night of spooks and horrors as children go door to door to ask for tricks or treats.

Or perhaps your family celebrates your ancestors for Día de Los Muertos (Day of the Dead) or Samhain, on October 31st.

B is for Bon Om Touk.

Also known as the water festival, Bon Om Touk is celebrated at the end of Cambodia's rainy season. The water in Tonle Sap Lake is now decreasing so the lakes neighbors gain land and celebrate with boat races.

C is for Christmas.

Christmas celebrates the Christian deity, Jesus, and the day he was born. In Christian belief, Jesus is said to have died on the cross for all sins and was resurrected three days later.

 is for Dongzhi.

Dongzhi is one of many celebrated on the winter solstice and serves as a reminder of the balance of light and dark in each of us, as well as everything around us.

 is for Eve.

The Eves of many saints are celebrated in this quarter of the year- St. Anne's, St. Catherine, St. Andrew, St. Barbara, St. Martin, St. Tibbs, St. Nicholas, St. Thomas.

F is for fireworks,

Fireworks can be seen worldwide on New Years' Eve, as people hope the new year will bring better prospects.

G is for Guru Nanak Jayanti.

Guru Nanak Jayanti is celebrated on the birthday of the founder of the Sikhi religion, Guru Nanak Dev Ji Gurpurab. Sikhism is a monotheistic belief celebrated by many people in several Indian communities.

H is for Hanukkah.

Hanukkah represents a seemingly impossible battle won by a small group of Jews. During the eight nights of celebration, the first candle is used to light each of the eight others each on their coinciding night, fried foods are eaten, dreidel is played, and coins are given to children to reward good behavior.

I is for Imbolc.

Imbolc is celebrated by Celtic Pagans, Wiccans, and Christians alike. This holiday celebrates Brigid, and warmer weather coming. During this time, bonfires and candles are lit, the weather is used to predict how long winter will last, and crosses to represent Brigid are made.

J is for Jesus.

Jesus was met by the three kings on Epiphany. The three kings traveled far to each give Jesus a gift of prized treasures- gold, frankincense, and myrrh.

K is for Kwanzaa.

- Umoja: Unity
- Kujichagulia: Self-determination
- Ujima: Collective Work & Responsibility
- Ujamaa: Cooperative Economics
- Nia: Purpose
- Kuumba: Creativity
- Imani: Faith

Kwanzaa is a celebration in recognition of African-American culture. Seven candles are lit on seven separate days, each with a principle to be remembered.

 is for Lorhi.

Lohri marks the end of the winter solstice in Northern India and is celebrated by tossing seeds and candies into holy bonfires while singing and dancing praises as a form of harvest ritual.

M is for Mardi Gras.

Mardi Gras takes place at the end of the 12 days of Christmas. During this time, there are parades, music, fireworks, and many other forms of celebration. These celebrations last until Fat Tuesday which is also the day before Ash Wednesday (A.K.A. Lent).

 is for Newtonmas.

Newtonmas celebrates the birthday of Isaac Newton, the founder of the three laws of physics. Newtonmas is celebrated as a secular, as well as scientific, alternative to Christmas.

Law 1:

What is in motion stays in motion.

Law 2:

Force equals mass times acceleration

Law 3:

For every action there is an equal and opposite reaction.

O is for oil lamps.

Oil lamps, called diyas, are burned during Diwali. This festival of light, in the Hindu culture, reminds the people to protect their inner own light.

P is for Pahos.

Pahos is a type of prayer stick that is made for Soyal. Soyal is another of many winter solstice celebrations and is observed by the Hopi and the Zuni peoples. On this day, dances are performed by warriors and powerful tribe members to coax the sun god to bring light, and with-it warmth, back to the people. It represents the second creation of life.

Q is for queen.

Queens and kings we all are on Saturnalia. Saturnalia has been intertwined in many traditions (such as where we get the "Christmas Tree") and is named for the Roman god, Saturn.

S is for Shakyamun.

Shakyamuni was the original name of the first Buddha, and he is celebrated on Bohdi day. There are many ways to celebrate Bohdi day, some choose to chant and meditate, some choose to read Buddhist texts, and others choose to spend the day helping others.

 is for Thanksgiving.

Thanksgiving or National Day of Mourning are two common choices to recognize on the fourth Thursday of November if you live in the United States.

 is for unwrap.

V is for virtual.

Unwrap those gifts of prosperity and abundance. Whether you celebrate in person, or virtually, there are many ways to celebrate the holidays.

W is for Winter Solstice.

Winter solstice is approaching and was a time for people of the northern hemisphere to choose whether to stick indoors and pray for the light to come again, or go outdoors and coax the light to come, but did you know in the southern hemisphere it is the opposite? The summer solstice (or Litha) is a time of the longest day of the year, and people begin to pray for the sun to become shorter and give cool air and rain so that all does not dry up and/or burn.

is for BoXing Day.

BoXing Day was originally meant to be a day to give to the poor, although some now refer to it as a shopping holiday.

Y is for Yule.

Yule is an ancient Germanic holiday celebrated around the winter solstice to celebrate rebirth and renewal. On this day, an altar is set, a Yule log is burned, feasting takes place, and the sun is "welcomed back".

 is for zero degrees.

Zero degrees is how some will describe the heart of Krampus. In some Germanic beliefs, this nightmarish horned figure is seen as a half-demon and is depicted as Santa's evil opposite that punishes naughty children during Christmastime.

www.ingramcontent.com/pod-product-compliance
Lightning Source LLC
Chambersburg PA
CBHW041813040426
42450CB00001B/24